Kicked In The Ass Hard, And Still Here

Jay Williams, PhD

Published by Frog Cottage Press, 2024.

KICKED IN THE ASS HARD, AND STILL HERE

First edition. March 5, 2024.

Copyright © 2024 Jay Williams, PhD.

ISBN: 979-8224499977

Written by Jay Williams, PhD.

For John

Now And Forever

MOLLY AND SAM

They waited at the stage door.
A man and a woman.
In love.
In their eighties.
And they had a story to tell me.
Seventy five years ago, they played together.
In Europe.
In a dusty yard, two little kids.
In a concentration camp.
Both Jewish.
Molly and Sam felt safe together.
When the camp was liberated, they got separated.
Both wound up in America.
Both married other people.
Both lost their spouses.
And then a miracle.
They met, once again.
They got married.
Molly showed me her arm.
The number from the camp was still on her arm.
Life is hard.
Then it is simple.
Life is good.
Then it is horrible.
Then it is good again.
Molly and Sam.
Sam and Molly.

They told me their story.
They were in love.
Still.

SIMPLICITY

I want to share with you some true moments that paved the way for change in my life and the life of people I knew.

Molly and Sam (I changed their names) were two of the fortunate Jewish people in Europe who made it out alive at the end of World War Two.

Most of the people you will meet in these pages did well, made it out of their varied "kick ass" moments in a powerful way.

A few were not as lucky.

Why another book about personal growth and transformation? I was determined to bring something new to this arena, this stage, this moment in my life, and in yours. What could that be?

I closed my eyes and it came to me: just tell the truth as I experienced it. Don't pad it with a lot of scientific jargon. Keep it simple.

And what could be more simple than the story of "The Red Balloon"? Quick view: a little boy, Pascal, in a French town was befriended by a balloon. It just arrived one day and became his companion until a bunch of jealous kids stomped on the balloon. Nasty. But kids will be kids.

Joy was there. Then utter sadness. Could there be a happy ending? You bet.

Picture this: a few balloons of brilliant colors floated into the streets. Then more and more balloons. The boy was covered in balloons and they scooped him up and he flew! Actually flew.

Joy returned.

And then it hit me.

There IS something new swirling around in my imagination that might help others.

When I am most vulnerable, clarity is mine for the taking. And with clarity comes personal power that changes my outlook.

It's like this: the Universe wants us to succeed. The little boy in "The Red Balloon" did not need a school room to teach that message.

The path delivering Pascal back to JOY opened for him. When that happens, and it does all the time, walk the path in the direction it takes you.

Simple. Simple. Simple.

Life can be wonderful.

Then life can be horrible.

Then life can be wonderful again.

Molly and Sam were the living proof of this.

As they stood next to me, holding hands, I felt compelled to tell their story some day. They were survivors: the lucky ones.

And then there are the unlucky ones.

Thus, I begin.

DOUG

One day in a busy city.
    A man cleared his desk.

He found his way to the top of a tall building.
    And jumped out the window.

His pain was too much.
    He was ready to leave.
    Was this sweet relief?
    I would like to think so.
    Doug was my friend.
    A caring, brilliant doctor.
    He was loved.
    I miss him.

DECIDING TO STAY

Charles had a gun in his pocket.

He was going back to his southern home.

To do harm to the male relative who had molested him as a young boy.

This "fire" within him was "shut up in his bones" as Charles had never told anyone his story. It was time to.

His momma sat on the step to the house.

She listened.

"Sometimes you just gotta leave it in the road."

Wise momma.

Charles got rid of the gun.

The fire slowly was extinguished.

He decided to stay.

These moments are from the contemporary opera "Fire Shut Up In My Bones" based on a memoir by Charles M. Blow, with music by Terence Blanchard and a libretto by Kasi Lemmons. More about this true story later.

WHY?

I was on the floor shouting and screaming, louder and louder. My brother had recently died at the age of 32. Why?

I was angry at myself and a bit angry with him.

On the edge, but not sure what to do about it.

Got it out. Out of my body and out of my head.

Silence. Gentle silence.

My eyes closed.

Someone put a strawberry in my mouth.

I decided to stay.

KICK ASS

Jim grabbed me by the arm, took me into the laundry room, slammed the door shut, and kicked me in the ass. Hard.

It was not a punishment, it was a gift.

Some fifty years later I still appreciate that moment. It was a wake up call for me. What a jerk I had been. Yes, I was receiving a lot of attention for my work on stage. So what.

And, yes, I was being an ass: the applause went to my head. I did feel vulnerable with Jim in that room. The vulnerability gave me amazing clarity. It is a lesson that has stayed with me. I needed a quick "fix". I got it.

Many years later I was on the deck of the Intrepid on the Hudson River in NYC doing a film, "National Treasure", with Nicolas Cage, being blown around by a helicopter over my head.

This was a scary moment as my body was being forced down an open staircase by the wind from the helicopter.

I kept holding on. I did not want to fall. And then the director wanted another "take", a better version of that scene. And he shouted "Back To One," That meant, get to your exact starting point so everything on screen would match. I went back to one and we did it again.

Back to one: each day we have the chance to go back to one, the place that allows us to reset our lives.

Mark Twain said "the most important days of our life are the day you are born and the day you find out why".

I was born in Newark, NJ and given the name Jay. and was probably a brat, as my brother labeled me from day one. The journey to "why" is still evolving, yet I travel on in a merry little way.

And so this book. I am a storyteller, a coach, a researcher with a PhD from New York University, and a very grateful guy. And I feel free. The PhD did not make me smart. People I knew and observed helped to do that.

Mel Robbins wrote a well-loved book, "The Five Second Rule" and my favorite quotation from that book is this: "If you are searching for that one person who will change your life, look in the mirror."

PAIN AIN'T PERMANENT

Now to us, this evolving journey, this call
to action for both of us.

I need to remember that kick in the ass each day so I do not get complacent. And it is no secret that the kicks we endure are often scary, maybe life threatening.

Yet, they should not, cannot, make us feel as if we are in prison. As a good friend said, "pain ain't permanent".

And let's celebrate something.

Albert Einstein was going on about life and the human body and related this: there's a one in 400 trillion chance we could be born.

So, stop whining about the small stuff: you and I were born. I embrace that as a miracle. And I am still very pleased to be here. Hope you are, too.

The writer C.S. Lewis spoke of friendships. "Friendship is born at that moment when one person says to another: 'What! You too? I thought I was the only one'".

Two things are evident here: we need to open up more and just "say it". Instant connections can allow us to experience a reawakening every day.

I love when I meet a stranger at the market or on a walk. I try to remember to smile. That usually leads to some form of chat. It can make my day. Little things mean a lot.All of those "what, you too?" moments help to reclaim our joy.

You will meet some people later in these pages who felt suffocated by life. Until they found a way to free themselves. Rumi was way ahead of me: this poet-sage from the 13th. Century wrote: "Why stay in prison when the door is wide open."

Ever watch a gerbil on the wheel? Round and round. Actually I do admire that gerbil. He has his own purpose, does not seem to be bored and is on a journey filled with action.

We should all be so lucky. And we can be.

You and I are still under construction, and with each building block there is a moment where we might find a wake up call. Perhaps we are screaming for help. Some of us find it, some of us do not.

It's a matter of action, and a matter of perspective.

Winston Churchill came up with a line that still resonates in a mighty way: "If you are going through hell, keep going." I would love to have a tee shirt with those eight words boldly printed. Just to see how people react.

MOONSTRUCK

"Moonstruck", the film, stars Nicolas Cage and Cher. Great team with amazing chemistry. "I have no life" screams Nic in one early scene. They play two people who just feel "dead". Until one day when they meet.

He takes her to his apartment. She makes him a steak. They go to his bed (yeah, they do the deed). She gets a makeover. Gorgeous.

They meet at the Metropolitan Opera House in Lincoln Center, NYC,sit in the best box seats and watch the opera "La Boheme". She cries. They fall in love at that moment. Walking afterward in the snow, they have found an amazing life once again. And, yes, they plan to marry. All in one day.

A fairy tale? No, it happens every day. Sometimes all it takes is to change your channel from a crappy show to an inspiring one. Remember that Mark Twain quote: the day you find out why?

The "Moonstruck" lovers found out why in one day. Sometimes it can happen in a minute.

ANOTHER SAM

You, perhaps, have seen the film about Sam called "Dodsworth". A self made man, manufacturer of automobiles, married to a shrewish lady, and he loves her. And then he realizes he can't stand her. He is faithful until she is not.

Sam and the wife plan a trip to Europe after he sells his company and he is comfortable for life

They get on the boat and then all hell breaks out. She doesn't like this, she doesn't like that. Yuck!

Sam is good looking, rich, personable and tired of the shrew. Yet he holds on and does everything to make her content. She will never be really happy; OK is the operative word for wifey.

Then Mrs. Dodsworth falls for a European guy, or two. Oh, this is what I have been wanting, she thinks. She carries on. And is still bored.

Sam, one day, encounters the most charming, warm lady who lives in Europe in a beautiful home overlooking the sea.

And he keeps his distance: he is married and faithful.

Mrs. D is not so faithful and has an affair with a well born European; his mother has to meet Mrs. D and takes an instant dislike to her. (A very insightful grand dame, she forbids her son from marrying the shrew.)

So, Mrs. D is dumped and makes plans to return to the USA with Sam. Sam agrees.

They get on the boat and the shrew begins to complain, immediately, about the "low class" people aboard the ship, the draft in the grand saloon, everything.

What would you do if you were Sam?

That's what he does.

He asks the steward to get his bag from his cabin, leaves his wife on the boat knowing she will have plenty of money and a true divorce ahead, and gets off the boat.

The last scene: the lady with whom Sam is truly in love is seen on her balcony looking very much alone.

Until she spots Sam in a small boat coming to her villa. She is ecstatic. They live happily ever after.

So, I remind you what LR Knost wrote: "Life is amazing. And then it's awful. And then it's amazing again." Pascal, the little boy in Paris with all of those balloons: this is the way it played out for him in just one day. Seize those moments of joy. They will come.

A SPECK OF DUST

A dream.

This happened exactly as follows: I was reading a book (in the dream) and a speck of dust fell out of the book. Just a boring speck. The speck just sat there on the floor. Until it became the smallest cat you have ever seen. A full cat, yes, but only an inch high.

The cat was majestic. Whiskers straight out, ears full and strong, a very long tail. This cat just looked up at me. With curiosity and with love.

You always know when a cat likes you (or does not). This cat liked me.

Very quickly,the cat found an open door and left on a journey, never to be seen by me again.

I woke up remembering every frame of that dream. And it was in color. And then I got it. (That elusive "IT" that is always in us, yet appears only when we go for IT, and welcome IT.)

John and I were married and together for 46 years. He "left his body" about two years before the dream (I do not embrace the word "died", just a personal choice).

Those of us who have been lucky to have "the love of our life" know how rare this can be.John and I had a great romance and one day I asked him why it had worked so well. He did not hesitate in his response: "because we are both curious about life". Wow. So simple.

The dream woke me up, one of those kick ass moments. Life goes on and we can take action to make it work or we can sit on our butts and be miserable. I chose to be OK and content. That is how I remain today.

And as you and I know, the path to anything is never easy or predictable. Yet it is OUR path. As Dylan Tomine wrote, "the path is the goal."

Every path leads somewhere. I like to think that it leads to a personal arena where anything can happen.

Sometimes it is good, sometimes not so good. Yet there is an event there, just waiting for you.

STARTING OVER

Bernard Pomerance wrote in the play, "The Elephant Man": "Sometimes I think my head is so big, because it is so full of dreams."

I started over because of that cat dream. I know the dream was sent to me by John. He was giving me consent to take action, grab hold of life, live it fully and move on.

And move out of NYC. I had been there a long time, right on West 57th. Street, the best place to live in NYC. So I moved to SW 58th. Place in Ocala, Florida.

Where the hell is Ocala? I hear that all the time from friends. It is north of Disneyland. From 57th. Street in NYC to 58th. Place in Ocala. Strange but true. And I like it here. A lot. I have a wooded property, a big cabin, and there are butterflies dancing about on the warm days.

Euphoric? No. OK, definitely.

TO PEE OR NOT TO PEE

I was in London with John on one of our many work or pleasure trips and had been upgraded to a suite and was more than content until I got up to pee in the middle of the night and fell asleep standing up.

I landed in the marble shower stall. The next morning I felt fine. Nothing broken, no blood, no obvious concussion. Lucky.

Back in NYC. Two weeks. And then crap happened. I was having balance issues, falling into walls, and then I could not walk.

Action was needed and fast. Took myself to the emergency room at Mount Sinai Hospital. Scans and more scans and then the news: I needed surgery, fast, if I were to live. I had no fear, no hesitation at all. Yes! Just do it.

Done.

CHEERLEADER

An angel named Chan was sitting at the foot of my bed. Chan said the following: "I am no longer your doctor. I am now your cheerleader." He had saved my life, along with his team.

Rehab for two weeks, I learned how to walk again, tie my shoes, button a shirt. Embrace the OK in life.

We can do it. It requires energy, focus and will power. The truth is, we are powerful.

That moment with Chan was one of the "why am I here" epiphanies: this life is not a dress rehearsal, it is now, to be savored. Push the reset button. Are we stuck at times? Surely we are.

And yet that is not the final view: it is not where you start, it's where you finish. Hold onto that.

PUTTING OUT A FIRE

"Fire Shut Up In My Bones" is the name of an opera. It is a brilliant piece of stagecraft and storytelling. No sopranos screaming high notes at us for hours (if you ever sat through a Wagner opera you will know what I am talking about).

Molested at a young age, it is the vivid retelling of what happened to a young boy living in the south. It is based on the life of Charles M.Blow, a New York Times writer. Charles was a kid when a male relative took away his innocence. He never told anyone.

Until he did.

Charles did well in college, found love with a woman, yet was so stuck, bottled up, that he almost relinquished his energy, his greatness, his will.

Until he decided to take action.

He got a gun. Took a journey back to his home.

Was going to do harm to the relative who had hurt him. But he stopped short of doing that.

When he got home, Momma was waiting on the steps of the simple house where Charles grew up.

And Momma spoke words to her son that I want you to read, and always remember: "sometimes you just gotta leave it in the road." Do me a favor: say those words out loud. Please.

SAY IT

The last moments of the opera find Charles and his Momma sitting on the step to the house.

Charles looks at her and, after years of holding it in, says to her, with great calm: "I have something to tell you." Quietly they enter the house. And the opera is over.

With the gun in his possession Charles almost acted in a way that would have landed him in prison for life, or worse. He opted out of that choice. He could have gone on for years holding in the trauma. Or he could do what he did: he opened up, big time, went home and told Momma his story.

Telling Momma the story was the best decision: choose the path that leads to healing and avoid the extremes of non action or dangerous action. I will get back to this later.

THE WAY

"When you start to walk on the way, the way appears": this is one of Rumi's most telling quotations. We are not alone. Ever. We have a mouth and most of us can speak. Whether we are heard is up to us.

The way, or the path, is paved with action. Otherwise it will be overgrown and lifeless.

Charles, in the opera story, was terrified by what had happened to him, so he "shut up" for so many years. Until he did what you and I have the ability to do: Say it! Tell it, Shout it out. Scream. But should I really do that?

"But" is a dangerous word. "But I can't tell my wife that her habits drive me bananas. I can't tell my husband to clean out the sink and not leave the dishes there, But the boss will dislike me if I fend off his sexual advances. But the neighbors will turn against me when I complain about their loud music."

We are just about to do something that could change our lives, open the path, release the fear and the "but" word plays in the brain. And it could ruin us. It is such a damaging word. "If I act and do something about how I feel, who I am, what I need, it could backfire, so I won't".

"I will just shut up and go on."

Sorry, it cannot work that way for people who want to escape their self-imposed "prison." There are no bars, no thick concrete walls, no loud banging doors. No crap.

Imagine this: you have a valve on the top of your head. This valve can be "opened". Take three fingers and lightly brush the top of your head. Do this in a circular fashion until you take the fingers away, gently.

Something escapes.

What has been swirling around in your monkey mind starts to leave. The noise in your head may quiet down. All the crap making you feel like a limp dishrag: be gone. Anger, be gone.

Resentment, be gone. What if: be gone. But, be gone. Silence may happen.

In a moment I will tell you the story of Betty.

But first a little background about how I found my backbone.

NO PICKET FENCES

When I was a kid, we had a school reader about Dick and Jane, their parents, and a dog. Life was bucolic living in a house with a white picket fence. Seemed ideal. Wow. People live like that?

Well, I didn't.

We had a small apartment. My father did all he could to put food on the table. One night he came home from the only job he could get at the time and tossed onto the dining table a hundred or so coins: money he had made that night from parking cars. I felt we were rich.

And then all hell broke loose as some infidelity took place; the bubble had burst.

Wake up call!

In my years of growing up, the bubble burst many times.

One night coming home from a date, my friend and I walked up to the apartment. Two guys came down from the floor above. Shiny big carving knives were placed on our throats.

I remember, vividly, not being scared and I knew not to move or resist. They got our gold school rings and wanted more. Suddenly a neighbor opened her door and the gentlemen ran out like squirrels.

The big deal in the theater district in NYC is 42nd Street. I was knocked to the ground, hands around my neck, being strangled. Cops came, saw this and did nothing.

I just got up and walked away. Breathing hard.

When my brother tried to kill me, I honestly do not remember much except to try and stop the bleeding and deal with it.

I'm still here.

Lost my mother, my brother, my father, my grandmother and my husband.

I'm still here.

Not so lucky: Dave was a talented performer who never could get enough sexual satisfaction or enough drugs. He was only in his 20's when he died of Aids.

Lydia (not her real name) had the life sucked out of her by some uncaring employer and took to alcohol. It made her feel alive. She did not make it and died when she consumed so much alcohol that her body shut down.

Thousands of stories, all real, that took lives.

As for me: I have never been molested, the knives did not enter my throat on the night we were mugged, my neck was not broken on 42nd Street and I am a cancer survivor and a brain surgery wonder kid.

I feel that I am being taken care of by some amazing power: is it God? Perhaps. Is it the Universe? Perhaps. Or is it pure determination to keep on keeping on. And not having the rug pulled out from under me.

I have learned not to be a doormat.

Later on I will share with you some stories from training events, masteries, workshops, and other life changing forums that allowed me to grow up fast.

I have enormous respect and empathy for those whose horrors never seem to go away. Pain is real. Being molested, raped: all too real. Having been thrown out of your home is real. Being bullied to the point of attempted suicide is real. Having incurable cancer is real.

VULNERABILITY=CLARITY

Vulnerability is always there, as anything could be lurking around the corner. Yet, for me, those little openings in the road that are really gifts, provide clarity. You can create the actions that make life OK. Or you can choose not to.

A fun little drawing.

This is us when we are OK, content, have it all sorted out. It is #1.

I did not say "happy" even though this face looks pretty happy. There is only one place to be: first place.

The frown face is not where you want to be. We all are there in the course of a day, we go from 1 to 2 to 1. Some jerk almost drives into us as we cross a street. Not a #1 moment. The boss wants us to work tonight and we have a hot date. Not a #1 moment. These things are transitory. The "so what" events. They go away.

What does not go away, until we let it and work at it with the help of others, are the awful things that do happen and can sink us. Until we find a way to turn it around. #2 is the event that has messed us up: we feel stuck in place, we do not see the "out" and we might want to quit. Wonderful. Horrible. Wonderful.

Things can change in a day, an hour, a minute. The little boy in Paris you met earlier: his life went from first place, to nowhere, and back to first place in one day. We all know it can happen. When we let it.

Never, never, never give up. Later I will tell you about "Frankie" who was weighed down with crap that had happened in life. Frankie thought life was over. Just the opposite: Frankie reclaimed her life.

I will show you exactly how this played out.

EDGE

Fear and stress need to take a hike.

In the hundreds of folks I have spoken with, listened to, shared healing time with, fear of "whatever" has kept many locked up in their bodies. It can cause us to hide, it can suck the life right out of us. And it is an element to be dumped.

Consider this: we might be pushed to the edge by anything, any day. Stop right there. Don't be taken in by that panic. It goes away, with time and with help.

Now, the other side of the edge: travel there if you choose. The edge has gifts to give. That kind of edge paints a kaleidoscope of possibilities. Embrace them.

Appolinaire came up with this idea a long time ago. Yes, we are afraid. Come to the edge. "I can't." Yes, you can. Just stay safely at that inviting edge. Stop and breathe it all in.

Come to the edge, don't go over it. I did that many times, and I "flew". And I'm still here. Stop, now, and give that a thought. You might smile.

FEAR: BULLDOZE IT

My take on fear is to confront it like a bulldozer: flatten it out, try to make it disappear. Not easy. It takes energy and enormous focus. And sometimes a clue to letting go of fear comes in the simplest way.

You can be sitting in a church, a temple, a buddhist retreat room and, all of a sudden, you get something that makes all the difference. One word. That is all it takes. And it may be at a time when you really need, badly, that life jacket.

My moment happened in an ashram, a meditation center, in the hills of New York state, one evening, late, when I was tired and a bit bored and the leader was going on and on, sometimes in a voice that was so smooth that I almost fell asleep.

CONSENT

Consent was the word. What? Wait! Ha? I could not wait until the session was over to go to the leader and speak, quietly and thrillingly, about the word consent.

Wow! My inner peace rose up like the proverbial phoenix. I was home. In my own body. I owned that moment.

And all of a sudden I had no weight on my shoulders. I wanted to go out in the night air and dance under the moon. So I did. Carefully as it was rather dark on the wood chip path to my room. But I danced!

Consent to do what? And feel what? Here is one takeaway: that I can let go of the haunting worry of not being enough. Of not doing enough.

Consent to go on and be totally OK, totally open to life. I am a good person. I give to others.

Consent to all of this and stop beating myself up.

The past is the past. The present is a gift to myself. Stop thinking. Stop questioning. Just accept it.

And I got this: have compassion for all those around us and what they might suffer, all they might need. Spread the idea of consent so that others might not fear physical and emotional scarring.

"It is OK to feel the way you do, and I am here to listen". They need a cheerleader; we need a cheerleader. Be that person. Just stop talking and really listen.

And when we come to the ending moments of life: give consent to let people go, and receive consent, with love, that we will be OK.

Because that is exactly what we share: we will both be OK. I have come to the conclusion that the "conclusion" can be a great comfort and relief to those who are about to leave. It can, and often is, a beautiful moment.

LIGHTEN UP A BIT

"Eat a live frog first thing in the morning and nothing worse will happen to you the rest of the day." Mark Twain.

"Fill what's empty. Empty what's full. Scratch where it itches." Alice Roosevelt Longworth.

"Balls" said my father. What? He was a very decent guy who never swore. And yet he made his point quite clearly. If something went wrong, and things always did, he just proclaimed the word "balls."

And the world was good again.

ONE IS AS ONE DOES

Doing something for yourself can make life not only tolerable but magnificent. And it takes focus.

I had a friend who was from Cuba; he taught a lot of workshops and often chastised participants with one word, "fuckus"! He was really saying "focus!".

You had to be there, and I was and I love the guy for making me "fuckus".

Workshops and events and seminars: there is something to get from all of them. When we shut up and listen. Or better yet get off our butts and get physical, if that is on the menu for the event.

MASTER YOUR ARENA

Mastery is an interesting word. And it is an even better process. Master chemistry, master algebra (I never did, and I could care less about algebra to this day.)

One of the silliest masteries was in geology: I respect geology, for those who love the field and practice it, and need it.

It was a rocky road for me. Pardon that: it's just that the mastery was all about rocks. I had to put my hand through a hole in a box, draw out a rock and tell the leader everything about that rock. The whole thing "sucked". I wanted out of this rocky arena.

And what, really, is this "arena" thing.

It was a concept of life well before Theodore Roosevelt gave his famous "arena" speech at his Presidential Inauguration many moons ago.

There are thousands of arenas and arena concepts (political arenas, cultural arenas, bullfighting rings, training and seminar spaces and more.)

The arena I write about is a very personal place: as simple as your garden, as complex as an operating room. It is yours. It can actually be a place to dream, a field where life becomes crystal clear, a nursing home for the latter years.

One thing is clear, as Roosevelt suggested: when you get to the arena, you might be kicked in the ass.

You show up. There are no guarantees. The reward is often clarity. You can see things better, perhaps for the first time.

Now to a mastery that changed my life at a time when I needed to wake up and figure out the best way to dissolve the crap that was holding me back from success.

Picture a small rectangular room with four corners.

Three of us in the room plus a trainer. I will tell you at the end of this about the three who needed the training, I was just one of them.

It was a Saturday afternoon in NYC at a training center for professional actors and those who wanted to achieve that status.

It was a cold day outside, and very hot inside.

Eleanor Roosevelt once wrote: "do one thing every day that scares you." We were about to be scared, humiliated, exhausted, and brought to the edge of our craft. That is what we signed up for and that is what we got.

It begins. And no bullshit is allowed. I am in one corner, M is in another, and J in another. The trainer begins: you cannot touch anyone, stay close to your spot and be real.

Need: say I need you.

I do. Looking at the others I try to show my need. I get more intense and more personal and louder. We are all expressing, vocally, that we need others. Not bad. So far.

Hate: say I hate you.

I begin and immediately the trainer bashes me vocally and he is not having it, does not believe me, wants to throw a chair at me, and this is not allowed. Louder I go and still no dice. "I hate you, I fucking hate you."

I was doing better, and getting hoarse as this is going on and on.

I explode into a tornado of hate, not knowing where it is coming from and not caring. Stomping around in my "space" and not striking out so I would hit anyone, but my arms and legs are wild. And my breathing is crazy.

I did not want to stop, while J and M were like rabid dogs in their corners.

Stop.

The last word we are given is love.

"I love you." "I love you." And I begin to cry.

I looked at M and I really felt love for him. Love for the room, love for myself, love for my brother, my mother, my father and for my husband.

I am a mess.

It goes on until we fall to our knees, panting. If an actor can have an emotional orgasm, this is it.

It's over.

And it is just beginning. An actor, an architect, a nurse, a teacher, a husband, a wife: our lives are full of unexpected moments. We are lucky to be alive and we are fully under construction. I was hoarse, OK, better, more connected to life and the Universe.

Mastery: for sure. Now to go out in the world and spread the word.

Oh, the other two in the room: M is Michael Bennett. He created the Broadway show,"A Chorus Line". He was a billionaire. He looked like any wiry guy on the street with his baseball cap and jeans. He won the Pulitzer Prize.

Michael supported my desire to get back in show business. I will always cherish his memory and the moment I looked at him and said "I love you." Because I did.

J was Jerry Stiller. A sweet, talented guy. He was married to Anne Meara and they created many hilarious comic events together. You may remember him from a late life success as a kind of grumpy older guy in the television hit show, "The King of Queens."

I loved watching him that weekend in the New York mastery. I learned so much from him.

Especially how to never, never give up.

The good things stay with us. What did I take away from that three day mastery: need, hate, love–three words that come up a lot in daily life.

The word not used in that workshop: fear.

We did not fear anything. We did not hide anything: we were emotionally naked and it felt terrific.

STORY ABOUT A BOX

And no bullshit was allowed. We were there to soar, and that cannot happen if we hide. Say it, do it.

One person could not get any of it. Kept hiding emotion and did not allow the path to open one bit. His door was locked, Period. That person kind of enjoyed having a secure bubble around his body.

Not allowed. The trainer did something I had never seen before. He challenged the guy to a moment of pain, a kick in the ass moment. No, he did not touch him. Yet, he changed the guy right in front of our eyes.

I do not recommend doing this without trained people around (or if you have any kind of health problem). Always check with your doctor when you are not sure if something is right for you. Remember that every "body" is different.

Here is what happened: a heavy wooden box was brought to the front, along with the resistant "trainee".

"Take the box and put it over your head and keep it there." "No!" yelled the trainee. "Do it!"

He held the box over his head.

And he kept it there.

And he looked like he wanted to kill the trainer and all of us in the room.

And suddenly, the facial expression changed to calm, the guy was breathing in a natural way, color came into his cheeks. And he was told to do his monologue or poem or song, or whatever he had prepared to share with us.

At first it was strained and annoyingly fake.

"Do it again" we all said, encouragingly.

He did.

All of a sudden this quiet, beautiful voice emerged. The box was still above his head.

And then, magic. We saw a new person.

Not hiding, no artifice, just pure life.

He had gotten back to one: that place we all can own when we allow it. Stripped away to the essence of our being. A child again, perhaps.

With no expectations. Except to be OK.

Powerful.

This was exactly the way it played out that day.

There can be no script for something like this.

There is no soap opera crap.

When you get back to one, picture this: you can almost see your bones.

What happens: instead of layering on a lot of stuff that is not needed, you are removing layers and layers of worry, fear, distrust, resentment, abuse to your body, abuse to others. Just holding on to the things that make you stronger.

Oh, how good it feels!

The box slowly came down.

It seemed that the guy with the box did not want to let it go. He just held it in his hands. Was he crying? I believe he was. He just looked at all of us in the room and seemed to be very grateful.

What's natural can be hard.

Yet, nature is an everlasting companion.

Full of unexpected joy.

THE U-HAUL

51

Not everyone is lucky enough to get back to #1.

Let's face it, when we are going back and forth from a clear path to a densely overgrown sloppy and unforgiving path, action is needed. A cheerleader helps. Simple daily acts of housekeeping can work wonders.

We do not thrive in a mess.

Do the dishes, make the bed, take out the garbage, declutter, clean your clothes, clean yourself: all of these simple jobs make you feel better.

When we feel better, we can see better. Simple. Call for a U-Haul. And while you are loading it with stuff you do not need or want, throw away some of your emotional baggage.

Keep open to possibilities. First place is yours for the taking, once you get clear on what you want to take. Sometimes it is easy. Sometimes it is not.

BETTY

54

Betty was beautiful: long blonde hair, slender, the brightest smile, married, a big diamond ring from her husband, two sons, vivacious, a leader in the temple women's group, a successful manager of a photo studio.

Her beef stew was always a hit, her gentle wisdom with her kids kept them on course, her friends loved being with her. An ideal woman with an ideal life.

And then it all went to hell.

Let's be honest: when things begin to fall apart there is often no warning, and if the warning light goes on we often ignore it.

Never ignore the warning light. Find out what is wrong and try to get it fixed.

Fixing is a central step in resetting our lives. And yet, the fix is often elusive as there are no rules to follow. Doctors are not gods: they attempt to "fix" stuff often with pills, and more pills. Or they might downplay a symptom when they should check out every possible cause for an ailment.

I come from a medical family and have the highest regard for the healers. Their job is more and more taxing, paperwork is overwhelming at times, and a lot of people in medicine are leaving the profession in droves.

So, Betty began to feel unwell. Her gut function was more and more erratic, her energy began to decline to the point that she simply would not leave the house in fear that she might have an "episode" while out and about.

A person does not have to leave the house to create an arena. You just need space and an activity of some kind.

Betty just sat.

Her father, who was a doctor, tried to help her, but he was cold and not a gut expert. (I do not believe in having treatment from a doctor in your family, but that is another story.)

Eventually the world turned against her, or so she thought.

In actuality, Betty turned off the world as she had known it. She shut out her friends, family, her husband, and her one remaining son. She became bi polar, stopped eating well, sat in her recliner all day, did not sleep well, got leukemia and passed away.

None of that should have happened.

Yet it did.

When I look at the life of Betty, there was no support system (her husband was already on the road to alcohol abuse and dementia). She felt lost, became bitter, reclusive. She would not talk to neighbors. She would not talk to anyone.

She would not talk to me.

If only she could have gone back to one, reset, change the channel.

You can do that at any age, with any medical condition, with any lifestyle. The back to one folks, often the survivors, have this in common: each day they push the reset button. The garbage from the day before is peeled away, like an onion, while new attitudes, new energy, new images, new hopes take over. They SEE a path.

The night Betty left her body, I was in the room with her, holding her hand. She looked beyond peaceful: she had come home.

And it dawned on me that a certain miracle happens when a person is ready to leave. At that moment, because anything is possible, you CAN get back to #1.

I want to believe that Betty felt an embracing set of arms around her, that she felt her path was clear, that she was a gift to the Universe.

Indeed, she was.

CATS!

Betty loved cats; at one time she had 14 of them.

My husband John and I arranged for the best seats in the Winter Garden Theatre on Broadway for the show "Cats".

Lights go down and cats come dancing down the aisle. One stopped right next to Betty and she patted that cat quite affectionately. She was in bliss.

Another time we took her to Disneyland in Florida. Mickey and Minnie took an instant liking to Betty. Her favorite was Grumpy. She just loved that guy. A funny, enduring moment.

When Betty passed and her service was held, I placed a "Cats" T shirt over her. And said goodbye.

As you might have guessed by now, Betty was my mother. I miss her a lot.

NO RIGHT, NO WRONG

Today is bright and beautiful.

The field is big and feels very much like an arena: so let's picture it that way. Sunflowers all over, butterflies roaming about, a gentle breeze makes you feel like dancing if you want to.

You choose a tree to sit near, but first you hug the tree. Rumi wrote: "Beyond the rightness or the wrongness there is a field. I'll meet you there."

Welcome to your personal field.

Sit down and eat a strawberry from your goodie basket. Close your eyes and really taste the sweetness of that treat. Drink in the sun. Be grateful: you are in a good place.

Your eyes remain closed.

Suddenly, out of nowhere comes your horse. He looks down to you and is still. You have never been on a horse. You want to ride. You mount him. Hold on, and begin to move. He will take you across the field gently and with calm resolve. Your sense of freedom, as you ride, is palpable.

Your body becomes a part of his body.

The energy is electric.

You ride and start breathing so fully that you might rise up to the sky. Ride more. Breathe more. Live more. Be a kid again.

Just be.

No cares. You are warm all over. As you breathe you let out sounds: you just let them come out of your body. Ah, Ah, faster they come, and the horse starts trotting quickly. You hold on.

Hold on, you are euphoric! You are completely aware of your magnificence. The horse slows down and brings you back to your tree.

You dismount carefully and look into the eyes of that gentle giant.

Still breathing in the most thrilling way. You pat your horse's neck slowly and with great care. He whinnies. And then trots away, never to be seen by you again.

YOU WAKE UP. The DREAM was real. Things have changed.

A butterfly is on your cheek.

THE PIGEON LADY

I first heard the F word when young, not in school or in the playground. Out of the mouth of a very sophisticated woman. Here she is.

She is standing in the Piazza San Marco in Venice, Italy.

She has a pigeon on her head.

The pigeon did not bother her at all.

Just another moment in a very colorful life.

And she was smiling.

Perhaps because of the passionate night she had just spent with her tour guide. Doing what comes naturally.

The lady had been married to a doctor who was 19 years her senior. They had two kids. He died.

Left her with nothing. He did not believe in insurance.

So, what to do? Action was required and she took it. Found a job in a medical facility and took a bus to work for 20 years. Never complained. She made it work.

Found that she could live in a swell apartment in a swanky neighborhood for very little money. Took herself to Europe, had a lovely affair with her tour guide. Brilliant.

Very few #2 moments in her life. Yes she lost her husband, both children, and her mobility.

Yet, this was the most stimulating woman I had ever known. She created a life that made her content.

And this is what I got from her (aside from the F word):

Live simply.

Be grateful for what you have.

Enjoy watching the Mets.

Do crossword puzzles daily.
Stroke a cat every now and then.
Say what you feel.
Connect with others.
Take risks.
Sleep well on soft sheets.
Eat hamburgers.
Eat brownies.
Drink lots of tea.
Don't be afraid of clowns.
"I am good enough."
Keep active.
Knit gifts and send them.
Don't be afraid of anything.
Show up.
Be a cheerleader.
Say "yes" to life.
Avoid pills except when essential.
Good genes help.
Never be nasty.
Try pot once; she did. Once was enough.
Be the conductor of life, not the caboose.
Say "I love you" often and mean it.
Be playful.
Life will kick you in the ass.
"This too shall pass."
Touch someone on the cheek.
We are not machines. Fix what needs fixing.
Open a new door, daily.
Declutter your space.

Listen more than you speak.
Be sexual as long as you can be.
Never be boring, to yourself or others.
Buy good clothes: they last.
Be like an onion: peel away the crap.
If you come to a "wall" walk through it.
If you get wet, it is not the end of the world.
See better even when you can't.
Never let the parade of life pass you by.
And so much more.
Her pathway: always forward.
Cover it with flower petals, not mud.

She lived to be 102.
Her name: Minna Strauss Fink.
My grandmother.
I wanted you to know her.

Here I go with a Jerry Herman moment.

A silly, yet funny lyric from the Broadway show "Mack And Mabel": "when a sky full of crap falls into your lap, just tap your troubles away."

The show did not fare well at the box office, but the tap number was a hoot. I still want to learn to tap dance. Why not? Action. That's the fun. And the challenge.

If we don't move, we lose (cannot remember who said that, yet you do not need to be an Einstein to embrace good, common sense).

Ever see one of those bright roadside signs for overnight lodging: Comfort Inn. Funny idea: do you want to stay in the Comfort Inn tonight or the Discomfort Inn. You get the point.

STRAWBERRY

A big ripe delicious strawberry was dangled over me, and placed in my mouth. Eyes were closed so not a clue who put it there. We had not eaten for many hours so this was a total treat.

Lying on a carpeted floor with about 200 others stretched out all over the room. Screaming at each other.

Total bedlam. It was time to heal.

Who is in the room?

Teachers, artists, professors, laundry attendants, mail carriers, doctors, former inmates from prison, grandmothers, divorcees, attorneys, famous and not famous, the accepting ones, the resistant ones, cancer patients and survivors, just regular folks seeking something.

No doubt, many believed they were in a form of "prison" in their lives, and saw no key to the door. One takeaway from this whole four day experience (known then as the EST training, Erhard Seminar Training) was this: the past is just that, it has passed.

The present can be your greatest present.

And we hear over and over again: "what is, is, what isn't, isn't." I'll buy that. I embraced it then, and I embrace it now, almost 47 years later as I write these words.

Let me stop and go back to Jerry Herman, a wonderful award-winning Broadway composer who wrote "Hello, Dolly!" and many other hit shows. Yet, it was Dolly that got my juices running whenever I saw it (about 30 times).

Dolly says to all of us: "I want to rejoin the human race before the parade passes by." A widow, she feels alone even with dozens of friends. She wants to feel totally alive once more and is a prime candidate for a re-awakening. So, she found a way to take steps to go back to one, and in doing so rediscovered her joy.

Imagine where you started in this life: being born with no clothes, no restraints, no expectations. And for most of us, no health conditions if we are born lucky (with "mazel" as some would say), and genes that will make us OK. Initially.

History will follow, yet for these first hours we don't have to do anything. Just be in the funny little baby bed, have a lot of doctors and nurses caring for us, be held by at least an adoring mother (daddy may or may not be there for many reasons), and just see the light. If we cry it is natural, unless it is not, and then the medical people could attend to that.

FLOOR TIME

So, here I am a lot of years after the "being born show", and I am OK. Lying on the floor with the strawberry in my mouth. Yummy.

And then all hell breaks loose as we are told, in this large training room in a very big New York City hotel, to look at the person next to us and scream at them.

It all feels very stupid. At first.

So I screamed something idiotic at the woman next to me (there were about two hundred in that room all over the carpet in every imaginable position.)

I probably started out quietly with "I hate you" or "get the fuck away from me". Who can remember. What I do remember is the total vocal chaos: shrieks, people sounding as it they were being attacked, knived, raped, spit on, crushed, and abandoned.

Many of those good folks had some of these things happen to them in the history of their lives, to this point. Many had no trauma, but everyone had issues.

One of my favorite definitions of the word "history" is in a play called "The History Boys" by Alan Bennett, and it is simple: "history is one fucking thing after another."

I love those seven words. Why? Because we have little control over the events that take place in our lives (our history) and many of those events truly suck.

So, we all keep screaming and losing our voices and being insanely child-like, adult-like, and wildly physical (while not touching anyone, which is a no no.) And then it all stops and we just stay on the floor. Quietly.

What happened could be thought of as a gigantic angry conversation with people we have not met.

We will know a lot of them before long.

In that room, with the good people who came there for the same reason I came there, it was akin to the night Jim kicked me in the ass in the laundry room.

KICK ASS REMINDERS

And, indeed, "kick ass" moments can often be life-changing gifts.

Please do not read into this that I am advocating the physical act of kicking someone hard. No way. What I do see is the benefit of the wake up you get when you most need it.

And all of us in that room paid to be there, of our own free will, and while there were rules (we could not leave the room except to pee or for an emergency or to take our pills,that kind of thing) we knew the rules in advance and accepted them.

"FUCKUS"

Remember my Cuban friend who wanted us all to focus in a workshop, but it came out "fuckus"? Funny, and true. Well, we were there and we focused all right. We paid the money and we wanted results.

And we showed up.

Well, most of us. Some had had enough after one of the four days, never to be seen again. If change is desired, if a new way to be on the path is a goal, then we better show up.

At work, in school, at home: we are better if we show up. "Be here now" many call it.

I knew I was in that room because of an incident in my history that I needed to "let go" of. And I did. I needed to release the questions about a death in my family.

My life was really good: I had a handsome and loving husband, a super good assistant professorship in a university, lived in NYC in a huge apartment (rent controlled, so easy to afford with two of us), a funny cat, some funky clothes, and very few issues.

Pain was very much evident in the training room, and when I listened, and listened well, I became more and more grateful that my life was pretty good.

The trainer listened to all of it, for four days. He was tall and handsome and confident and did not put up with bullshit. He was being paid good money to do a job and he did it.

FRANKIE

"Frankie" was in the room ("Frankie" is a composite of many, just so you know.)

She/he was the queen/king of the daytime soaps, and had many issues. I looked at her/him and got that Frankie felt lost, abandoned, inferior, a victim, at a dead end, and feeling like crap.

And it was totally real. Frankie was ready to explode.

It was not easy in that room with the trainer yelling at us: "wake up assholes." This was a constant in the first and second day of the four day experience. And it was wonderful.

We did not want to be coddled and stroked. We needed tough love and we got it.

Remember that word "it". I will get back to it.

What are you hiding? That came up a lot. We could not hide here: Not allowed. Some might call what happened in the room verbal abuse.

I like to remember it differently: the trainer was full of love for all of us, but it was certainly tough love.

Frankie was so interested in impressing people with various traumatic life events and the trainer was having none of it. "My mother hated me, I have no friends, I was abandoned as a kid," and on and on. It was real. Yet where was it real? Was that "right now" real, or past history real.

Yet, Frankie was in pain. And it needed to go away, take a hike. Clearly, the path needed to open. How to do that?

What Frankie and I got in those four days was this: there is nothing to get. "What is, is and what isn't,isn't" they told us. Is the pain there right now? There are elements of the pain that linger, perhaps, but the pain is from the past, not the now.

We were told we had to get "it." Yet "it" was inside us all along. So, there was nothing to get: we already had it. And what a powerful thing that "it" is.

Not only get it, embrace it: and when, years or moments from now, someone we love needs the "it", show that person the way. Sharing is a key to gratitude, and gratitude really matters.

This may seem very strange or confusing. Just wait. Something magical is about to happen.

What follows is a composite I developed from dozens of workshops, meetings, coaching sessions, intensives and masteries. A "Frankie" existed in all of those places. And a Frankie can be straight or gay, black or white or any background, religious or spiritual or a non believer, Just another person seeking something.

Just like you or me.

Frankie: "My mother hated me and threw me out."

Question: "What do you mean by that?"

Frankie: "She made me live with someone else, and I hated it."

Question: "What happened at home with your mother?"

Frankie: "What do you mean?"

Question: "Were you abused?"

Frankie: "No."

Question: "Did you have food and clothing and a nice room?"

Frankie: "Yes."

Question: "Do you still hate your mother for what happened?"

Frankie: "It was awful."

Question: "You are hiding from my question."

Frankie: "It was awful. She hated me."

Question: "You are being an asshole right now. Just Stop It. Ask this: was your mother equipped to give you a good upbringing, could she cope with being the mother she wanted to be for you?"

Frankie: "I don't know what you are saying. Just leave me alone."

Question: "Stop hiding. Answer my question. Did she ever hit you?"

Frankie: "Never."

Question: "Did you have a bed to sleep in and food on the table?"

Frankie: "Yes, but so what?"

Question: "What was going on in your mother's life and where was your father?"

Frankie: "My father was gone and I never knew him. They were divorced. It was just my mother and she hated me."

Question: "Did she have enough income to take care of you? Was she able to cope with you– without going over the edge.?"

Frankie: "I don't know about any of that."

Question: "You don't know or you don't want to know?"

Frankie: "I don't need this from you."

Question: "Is it possible you were loved by your mother and could not feel it at the time."

Frankie: "What do you mean?"

Question: "Sometimes we are given love in strange ways. Your mother may have done you the biggest favor by having you live somewhere else.

Did you ever consider that? And before you answer, how is your life today? Are you OK with feeling better about your mother- right now?

Are you willing to chisel away some of your resentment and create a new you. Are you?"

Frankie Says nothing.

Question: "Do you feel the same as you did 10 minutes ago?"

Frankie: "I don't know."

Question: "Has anything changed?"

Frankie: "I just don't want the fucking pain anymore. I can't stand the pain."

Question: "Did your mother hate you.?"

Frankie: Hesitates, looks around, and begins to cry quietly. "I just want this to stop."

Question: "Can you look at all of us and say to your mother: I love you."

Frankie: Shaking and not answering.

Question: "Do it!"

Frankie: "Mama, I'm sorry."

Question: "Go on."

Frankie: "I love you Mama. I love you."

Was there a "Frankie"? Damn right, but her/his name was not Frankie. It might have been Phyllis, or Eduardo or Joe, or Sam or Tasha, or Ben: it doesn't matter.

I know this: I have been there. I was feeling similar emotions, not in pain, per se, yet in a state of flux: and I have needed closure for things that happened in life. Was I entitled to that closure? Was I entitled to a clearer path?

Yes! And along with others, my life changed.

And that was more than I could have ever expected.

TRAINS

You and I are the conductors, the architects, the cheerleaders of our lives. Don't expect anyone to be as powerful in your history as you can be. I know this: I want to be the powerful engine, not the tired caboose.

There was a sense of euphoria at the graduation that took place on the final day of four.

Flowers arrived in the hands of our loved ones, and "Frankie" was glowing. I remember people who had looked so uptight in their business attire now wearing jeans, tshirts, no make up, no artifice. We were all more than OK. We had gotten "it."

I had cleared my personal path: To love others, yes, and to love myself first (back to one). And oh, so grateful. And what I also got was that the aim of my life was not to be "happy" but to be fully alive.

Just picture about two hundred of us, the graduates, hugging, with the most palpable feeling of freedom imaginable. Truly, some got out of their self-imposed prison cells in those four days.

What is in the way of getting your life back, or at least better. Are you holding on to your past history? Imagine standing in front of a mirror and not being happy with what you see.

Now, get out of the house and find a stranger to speak with. What do you learn from that stranger?

I was sitting with Alicia in a hospital emergency room while we both awaited test results. We shared. She wanted to start anew and go with her child (she was a single mother) to Tennessee. There was nothing standing in her way, except doing it.

We supported one another on the journey and exchanged email addresses. That night she wrote to me: "you will never know how much you helped me." Wow. Back at you, Alicia. Our chat helped me, too: I was not "thinking" about my health issue, just about how decent life could be.

BIG JOE

Many moons ago there was a strange late night radio show called "Big Joe's Happiness Exchange." (Some may be saying "what's a radio, Jay"). Look it up on google. All we had to do was listen, not watch, and there were no commercials about pills and accident attorneys and the like.

So, Big Joe listened to stories: people called in and needed a new washing machine or a tooth or a motor for the car. Presto: listeners sent money and the new tooth was assured.

What is the point? We need to be grateful for what we have, forget about what we don't have, fix what is broken, get rid of crap.

Exchange happiness, or OK ness. "Make someone happy and you will be happy too" (a useful set of lyrics from the Broadway show "Do, Re, Mi.")

Connect. Be compassionate. Be grateful.

As for Jay: I do not want it all. I have enough. I am enough. Aside from not being able to see very well in my right eye (I have a bit of Bell's Palsy right now), that too shall pass as my grandmother often told me. And she was so right.

FEELING NEW

So, what is to be made of what went on during those four days in that hotel room almost forty seven years ago.

First, I did not want to do it, and when the introductory session was held, my husband John, who had previously done the training, asked me to go to the meeting. I brought no money and no credit card to pay for it. John was way ahead of me and brought the money. It was the best investment we could have made.

Here I go with Eleanor Roosevelt again: "do one thing every day that scares you." A very smart lady.

In that big hotel room with the overdone carpet, we could all feel safe. Almost everyone was polite. They just were. And this is what happened in the safety of the room with almost 200 total strangers: we said things that, perhaps, we had never said before. With each "opening up" that took place. There was no place to hide. Free from judgments, we could just be ourselves, together.

And we took off the masks. We got kicked in the ass a lot: nothing physical, but you get the point.

Just thinking about the types of "kicks" we get as the journey evolves. Once I worked with someone who was very talented. And then he got "kicked in the ass" by a newspaper jerk in a review.

Well, Mr Newsman: you did him a favor. He was determined to be the absolute best he could be. He got more training, he soared, he loved what he did. His success in NYC led from one Broadway show to another. Way to go,

I have said it before in these pages: when we are most vulnerable, we find the most clarity. The clarity might be disturbing at first, yet a little disturbance to the "usual" can work wonders.

ON THE EDGE

Screaming is a useful act when we are in emotional or physical pain. And yet, how many of us have ever screamed out?

One of the nice things about living in New York City was the underground subway system.

The subway was gross a lot of the time. And there were plenty of strange people lurking about. I went there once because I wanted to vent about something. The subway car roared into the station and it was my turn: I screamed big time. No one cared. No one even looked. It was a moment of total liberation.

A memorable British film exists called "Mrs. Henderson Presents", the lady of the title played by Dame Judi Dench. Mrs. H has just lost her husband; she was crazy about him. He was rich and left her very well positioned for the rest of her life. Now what?

After the funeral, she took herself out in a boat on a misty lake and screamed at the top of her lungs. She needed that release. She got it.

In the four day training, we all were on the floor screaming. At first it was odd. And then it seemed to be the most natural act imaginable.

As I screamed and relaxed more into the moment, I let things go.

We all had a reason to be in that hotel room in NYC. Mrs H had a good reason to be in that boat. We do what we need to do. And we row forward.

RICHARD

At only 32 he had left his body. We never found out quite why as no autopsy was desired by the family. Richard, a brilliant scientist and researcher, was my only brother. He was also gay and found a wonderful guy in California, so he moved there.

At the time of the four day training in NYC, I had just experienced this loss: and loss was new to me.

It just was. Yet I had never given myself the chance to grieve, to be angry at myself for not being able to prevent what happened. I was angry: but not just with myself. I felt angry with Richard. I was filled with fury about what had happened.

And I was screaming on that floor in that big room with so many others letting go, I may have cried. And I did let go. I loved Richard, he loved me, and life happens. Get over it. It was a moment of clarity: there is no fault, there is no regret, there is no "what if".

What there is, came to me fully that day: we have a clear path to gratitude: be grateful for what he brought to my life and to the lives of others. And I am.

Many people experience similar seminars, workshops, group discussions in church or the temple or the zen meet-up space and feel exactly the same way: gratitude for what we have learned, for the path that opened up so strongly, for the sharing from others, the freedom to just "say it". And the wow moment:"oh, you too?"

Confronting the demons: when we do that, all of a sudden the demons start, gradually or immediately, to disappear. When we get to a solid wall with no escape, we can walk through the wall. Think about it. We can do it.

I love this one image from a Hollywood film: a couple with problems comes to a wall. It seems impenetrable. They feel trapped.

All of a sudden the wall is gone: it was a fake, painted wall on rollers. The studio techies just rolled this enormous wall away and there was a field: the problem disappeared. It never was there in the first place.

LIFE'S A BANQUET
OR IT ISN'T

AS you have probably gotten by now, film has been a constant in my life ever since I was 13 and saw Rosalind Russell in "Auntie Mame". Mame was a wild woman: she loved excess, decor changes, men, fashion, travel. She met Beau and fell in love. He died. She went on. "Life's a banquet" she gaily said, "and most poor suckers are starving to death."

At age 13 I had no idea why I liked this woman. At 78 (when I typed these words) I found out: I wanted to be her. No, there was no interest in changing my sex: I loved being a boy (especially what boys find out about their bodies when they are around 13).

The key was Mame's freedom, her joy, and when there was the inevitable pain, how to take action and let it go.

Charles Foster Kane was a very different case.

Orson Welles (great director and actor) brought to life the story of CF Kane in the film "Citizen Kane."

Charlie, as some called him, had it all: smart (when he was), strong, entrepreneurial, rich.

So what. The more he lived, the more stuff he accumulated, the more miserable he became: to himself and to others.

He collected two wives.

One finally left him and the other wife he manipulated in such a way that she lost any sense of who she was. Until she also left him to live alone in that enormous, cold mansion.

He had millions of dollars of junk and treasure sitting in a gigantic basement. So what?

He had everything and he had nothing. We have heard that before. Mr. Kane had become a hostage; he did it to himself.

If only. If only he could go back to ONE when he, as a kid, had no money, no aspirations, no needs except one thing: to have those boyish moments on his sled that was named Rosebud.

When you watch the film, and I hope that you will, pay close attention to a final scene in the basement with a roaring fire in the chimney.

That's all I will say.

ONE

"One" is a magical position in our lives. Let's all go back there when given the opportunity: simplicity, clarity, little or no fear of anything, no need to hide, and no buts.

The word "but" is a roadblock. We can quickly wind up in #2 land: stuck, lifeless, feeling defeated, nowhere to go, limp dishrag territory. We need an anchor, not a roadblock.

We put ourselves there; don't blame others. "Oh, but my husband is a slob and it gets worse everyday. I know I need to change, but my wife did this! But the boss keeps putting his hands all over me. But what am I to do?" Stop with the buts. There is another word that will help: the word is ACTION.

I love the moment in the film "Fried Green Tomatoes" when Kathy Bates lets go of "but" and becomes her own woman: gets a good job, makes her own money, gets a makeover, finds joy in her own power. And let's hubby know that this is a new "channel" in life and he needs to deal with it.

We are not meant to be anyone's punching bag. Just not acceptable.

GOLD

There is a wonderful Christmas story about a single father and his daughter.

It is Christmas Eve and the boss tells dad, call him Brad, that he has to work late and finish the invoices or he will lose his job. This, on Christmas Eve: a bit of Scrooge in that boss.

Sarah, his daughter is home late at night, and has wrapped a gift for Dad: beautiful gold wrapping paper, expensive looking.

Sarah is a pretty great kid at age 11 or so. Even without a mother in the house.

The next morning, Sarah is opening her gifts and there is one left under the tree. Dad opens the gold wrapped box and almost explodes in anger: "Don't you know when you wrap a package with expensive paper which we cannot afford, you need to put something in the box?" Silence.

Sarah answers calmly: " Dad, there is something in there: I blew dozens of kisses into the box for you."

Dad is almost in tears and says to Sarah: "this is the best gift anyone has ever given me. I love you."

"I love you Dad."

ROSES IN THE GARBAGE

John Wooden: "Things turn out best for people who make the best of the way things turn out."

My husband John wrote to me once and this is what he said: "The worst truckload of garbage can have a beautiful rose in the middle."

Is it any wonder why I loved him so very much?

He also wrote this: "I am happy when I am kind to others, and unhappy when I am not."

I did something very stupid one morning. The sink was still full of dishes. I should have just "done" them, instead I got angry and stormed out of the house, being too vocal about the dishes. I cooked and John did the dishes. That was the unwritten plan.

I stayed away a good part of the day. Fear took over: will he let me back into the house, will he want a divorce, how can I make this right.

When I got home, John just did what John did: he put his arms around me and hugged me; that is what people who love do.

I never asked him to do the dishes ever again. I was, at that hugging moment, grateful for everything the Universe had given me.

And I found out that I love doing dishes. Still, to this day, I do not use my dishwasher. You could say that I am "odd" that way. Life goes where it needs to go when we let it.

GRATEFUL

You know by now that theater provided many of the best moments in my life, both on stage and off. I made a damn good living acting in Broadway shows on tour, some smaller shows in NYC, and other gigs.

Irving Berlin did a show called "Annie Get Your Gun". It starred Ethel Merman who was very loud, onstage and off. I thought she was swell; others had different opinions. Berlin wrote: "Got no checkbooks, got no banks, still I'd like to express my thanks, I got the sun in the morning and the moon at night." That's all. And that's plenty.

APPLAUSE

In a moment, there will be a "graduation" speech I have written just for you. After all, you have read this book. You deserve a graduation speech. First, a few words of gratitude.

I begin with a thank you to Franklin J. Ruck. Frank owned my house in Ocala in the "woods" as I call it because I am surrounded by majestic, mature oak trees. Frank loved those trees and the flowers he planted and the butterflies dancing in the back garden.

And he was loved by the many ladies to whom he would bring some of those pretty flowers. He was a gentleman in the true old fashioned sense. An Army man. And a hero.

Frank was on Normandy Beach the day the troops began the action that was, eventually, to end World War Two. He was awarded the Victory Medal. He and his wife Bernie were high school sweethearts. They filled my house with love. I feel it each day.

If this book is good at all, it is because I had this perfect house to write in. There are no sounds except the occasional crow,or the garbage truck twice a week. Otherwise, silence. It is my arena.

Being grateful: it makes all the difference. We wake up, reset, change the channel, and even if we are feeling like crap, take a breath and "see" those who made life good, really good, and the lousy mood can change.

I am grateful to Betty for taking me to the ocean one day: that started a lifelong love for the "great big blue pill." And Betty always reminded me to write thank you notes. I choose to remember her as a stunningly beautiful lady because she was.

My dad built me the best lemonade stand ever.

And he loved to play with my hair: when he did that, we laughed like crazy people. Crazy can be good at times. He never judged me in any way.

He loved me and he loved my husband John, just like another son. He stayed active until dementia took over. And even then, he loved women! I know because he had a "girlfriend" in his assisted living home. That's all I will say!

Minna got me my first job on a big Broadway stage in New York City.

Talk about losing inhibitions: I was naked in the dressing room with forty other guys as I applied thick dark liquid makeup all over my body. I did not mind it at all.

When the curtain went up and there were three thousand people watching, it did not scare me in the least. I was home.

My husband John was one of the few people who totally "got me".

He kept my path clear because the path was filled with love and acceptance. Not fear. He was the most fearless person I ever knew. Thanks, my darling, for never throwing me out. We were so curious about life: that is what made it work.

Grace taught me the word "why.". Strangely, when I got that lesson at the age of nine it let me relax and see all of the amazing possibilities in life. "Anything can happen if you let it" (Mary Poppins). And look, Ma, Mary could fly!

The football team at Long Branch High School.

Why? Let's just say that those magnificent black guys adopted me, kept me from being bullied, made me feel like the man I would become, and cleared my path which had been filled with self-doubt.

Sometimes, it just takes a team.

And hundreds of family members and clear-eyed friends all over the globe.

A true friend is one who will not let you sink.

One who will show up at the hospital to take you home after a life threatening experience, as did my special friend Donald.

And sometimes that friend is called Jim, and he will kick you in the butt when you need it. And then go off and play his guitar.

YOUR TURN

Close your eyes. Breathe. Feel as if you are floating on a cloud. Hold onto that bliss.

Go back to one: that place where you find a new, sturdy building block each day with nothing in your way.

Arenas are built with bricks, stones, sand, or just air.

Please believe that you can create an arena in a space you have, a dream you remember, a painting you bring to life, an operating room, a garden, a thousand other things.

Remember and hold dear:

The teacher who helped you find yourself.

The relative who let you be yourself.

The time you felt most alive and happy.

A friend who walked with you.

The feeling of being well after being unwell.

The time you got lost, and then found the path.

When you first felt sexually alive.

Falling in love, the first time.

Knowing you liked girls, a lot.

Knowing you liked boys, a lot.

Knowing you liked yourself, a lot.

When you almost died, but you lived.

Getting married.

Having your first child.

And maybe your second.

And maybe your third.

And being a grandparent.
And knowing you are still here.

IDA AND ISIDOR

Hello graduates. I start with a story.

"Still" is a powerful word.

When the Titanic was sinking (in the Broadway musical version), Ida and Isidor Straus were drinking champagne on the deck as the ship began to go down.

Still in love after a lifetime together, the pair refused to separate. She could have gone into a lifeboat (women and children first). That was not her style. The couple renewed their wedding vows, he broke the champagne glass with his foot (A Jewish wedding tradition), and they sang of their love.

Together, forever.

Life is really very simple. Get up, make your bed, brush your teeth, push the reset button not the snooze button, and ask this simple question: why am I here?

Go out, connect, and learn from others. Be grateful. Why make it so complicated? The comedian Groucho Marx was no fool: He said that "a black cat crossing your path signifies that the animal is going somewhere." Perfect. A pompous professor might have gone on to write an idiotic book about that cat. It was what it was. That's all.

Kiss: keep it simple, silly. And above all, keep it lubricated. What? Keep your road forward lubricated so it is easy to travel. Pave it with flowers, not mud.

At the end of the four day training event in New York City, we were given a little brown booklet. One of the

Werner Erhard sayings was "ride the horse in the direction he's going." You get the point.

You do not need a PhD to have common sense. Just keep it real. Buddha reminded us to be ready to accept the worst. He wrote that pain is certain, but suffering is optional. Fix what might be broken. Clean out the pipes.

Take small steps, one at a time. Just take them; no "buts" allowed. Go somewhere and connect daily: maybe just out to a garden, a stream, find a tree you like and hug that tree, and listen to what the tree is saying to you.

What the stones are saying to you. What the water is saying to you.

William Shakespeare was quite a guy. He wrote:

"And this, our life, exempt from public haunt, finds tongues in trees, sermons in stones, books in the running brooks, and good in everything. And I would not change it."

Keep your sense of humor. Laughter is a mighty good friend.

Television personality Ellen DeGeneres was a funny lady.

She told this story: "my grandmother started walking five miles a day when she was sixty. She's ninety seven now and we don't know where the hell she is."

"I am an old man," wrote Mark Twain, "and have known a great many troubles, but most of them never happened."

And hold dear the word still.

I almost died several times. I'm still here.

My brother tried to kill me. I'm still here.

I couldn't walk. I walked again. I'm still here.

I was being choked on Forty Second Street. I'm still here.

Yes, there was a knife on my throat. I'm still here.

My husband left his body. I'm still here. And that's exactly what he wished for me. To go onward. Spread the words that can heal, reclaim our joy. Just "pass it on."

Along the way we develop more strength, more passion, more clarity when we acknowledge the truth that we are vulnerable. That does not mean we are door mats.

No. We are all under construction as we get to "one" and build again. "Frankie" showed us that.

SAMMIE

One last story about a man named Sammie.
A handsome guy with bright, beautiful eyes.
At seventeen he did something awful to someone else.
It's not important what he did. It happened.

Sixty six years later he was still in a miserable prison cell, a lousy toilet and sink, heavy bars in front of his face, loud metal doors banging shut all the time.

He had a wish: to get out and do some good in the world. That's all he thought about. Not to be. Sammie died in prison. At the age of eighty-three.

Sammie once went to the edge and something lurking inside pushed him over: it was too late to go back.

He could not leave the prison walls. He did not walk the path at a high school graduation. He could not go out with a gal on date night. He did not have kids or grandkids. Yet he retained hope. A lot to be learned from the life of Sammie Robinson.

MAZEL

Remember that field I took you to?

With the butterfly on your cheek.

I think about that field a lot.

And how lucky I am.

Truly amazing.

Once again, I think of Molly and Sam at the stage door one night when I was playing on tour in the Broadway Show "Cabaret".

Onstage, near the end of each performance, I gave two oranges to my friend Sally Bowles and said: "I wish you mazel."

Mazel means luck.

I wish you mazel.

And I thank you for reading.

ABOUT THE AUTHOR

Jay Williams is an award-winning actor and director, a coach, cheerleader and writer of four books including the memoir "Finding Myself At The Stage Door." PhD from NYU, Kean University Laureate Professor. Just a simple guy with a lot of big oak trees in his backyard, a bunch of butterflies dancing about, and a gentle breeze to cool the afternoon. He spends time in London, England and Ocala, Florida. jaytsw@gmail.com

Photo By Topher Frog.
Cover Design By Daniel Eyenegho